Alabama

Revised and Updated

by Patricia K. Kummer

Content Consultant:
Allen Cronenberg, Historian
Arts and Humanities Center
Auburn University

CAPSTONE PRESS

Mankato, Minnesota

Capstone Books are published by Capstone Press
151 Good Counsel Drive, P.O. Box 669, Mankato, Minnesota 56002
http://www.capstone-press.com

Library of Congress Cataloging-in-Publication Data
Kummer, Patricia K.
    Alabama / by Patricia K. Kummer.—Rev. and updated ed.
    p. cm. —(One nation)
    Includes bibliographical references (p. 45) and index.
    Summary: Provides an overview of the state of Alabama, covering its history, geography, economy, people, and points of interest.
    ISBN 0-7368-1225-3 (hardcover)
    1. Alabama—Juvenile literature. [1. Alabama.] I. Title. II. Series.
F326.3 .K86   2003
976.1—dc21   2001047790

Editorial Credits

Jennifer Schonborn, series cover and title page designer; Juliette Peters, book cover designer; Patricia Isaacs, map illustrator

Photo Credits

Alabama Bureau of Tourism and Travel, 12, 16, 18, 21, 22, 25, 26, 29, 34
Alabama Forestry Commission/Kim Gilliand, 5 (right)
Capstone Press, 4 (left)
Corbis/Raymond Gehman, cover
International Stock/Jeff Greenberg, 30
Root Resources/C. Postmus, 4 (right)
James P. Rowan, 33
Unicorn Stock/Les Van, 5 (left); Jeff Greenberg, 6, 8, 10

1 2 3 4 5 6 07 06 05 04 03

Table of Contents

Fast Facts about Alabama 4

Chapter 1 Rocket City, U.S.A. 7

Chapter 2 The Land 11

Chapter 3 The People 17

Chapter 4 Alabama History 23

Chapter 5 Alabama Business 31

Chapter 6 Seeing the Sights........................... 35

Alabama Time Line 40

Famous Alabamans... 42

Words to Know... 44

To Learn More... 45

Useful Addresses 46

Internet Sites... 47

Index 48

Fast Facts about Alabama

State Flag

Location: Southeastern United States, along the Gulf Coast

Size: 52,237 square miles (135,293 square kilometers)

Population: 4,447,100 (2000 U.S. Census Bureau)

Capital: Montgomery

Date admitted to the Union: December 14, 1819; the 22nd state

Yellowhammer

Camellia

Largest cities:
Birmingham,
Montgomery,
Mobile,
Huntsville,
Tuscaloosa,
Hoover,
Dothan,
Decatur,
Auburn,
Gadsden

Nickname: The Heart
of Dixie
State bird: Yellowhammer
State flower: Camellia
State tree: Longleaf
State song: "Alabama" by
Julia S. Tutwiler and
Edna Goeckel Gussen

Longleaf

Chapter 1
Rocket City, U.S.A.

Huntsville, Alabama, is called Rocket City, U.S.A. The Marshall Space Flight Center is there. Its scientists invented the Saturn V rocket. This rocket carried the first astronauts to the moon.

Huntsville is also home to the Space and Rocket Center. This is Alabama's most popular place to visit. It is also the largest space museum in the world.

The museum has about 60 exhibits. Visitors can sit in a space capsule. They can touch moon rocks. They can see a moon buggy.

Huntsville is called Rocket City, U.S.A., because it has many space-related things to see.

Children can attend a space camp at the Space and Rocket Center.

Rocket Park is outside the museum. There, a Saturn V rocket lies on its side. The rocket is as long as a football field. Visitors can ride the Lunar Odyssey. This machine gives the feeling of lifting off into space.

Space Camp is part of the space museum. Children and adults can attend the camp for a week. Campers learn what it is like to be an astronaut. They wear space suits. They use real space equipment. Campers even fly a mock space shuttle mission.

The Heart of Dixie

Alabama is called the Heart of Dixie. Dixie is another name for the South. In 1861, 11 southern states seceded from the United States. These states formed their own country. It was called the Confederate States of America. Montgomery was the Confederacy's first capital.

Alabama is also the birthplace of the civil rights movement. Civil rights means that all people should have the same freedom and equal treatment by law. Important events took place in Montgomery, Selma, and Birmingham. African Americans worked for their rights in those cities. It was a hard fight. Many people did not want African Americans to be treated as equals.

Today, Montgomery is home to the Civil Rights Memorial. It names the people who died working for civil rights. Their actions increased civil rights for all Americans.

Chapter 2
The Land

Alabama is in the southeastern United States. It is part of a region called the Deep South. The Deep South is the southeastern United States.

Four other southern states are Alabama's neighbors. Mississippi is to the west. Tennessee is to the north. Georgia lies to the east. Florida is to the south and east.

Alabama's Water Boundaries

The Gulf of Mexico touches Alabama's southwestern corner. This makes Alabama a Gulf Coast state, also. Mobile Bay and Perdido Bay are along the coast. Dauphin Island lies south of Mobile Bay.

Mobile Bay is one of Alabama's water boundaries.

The Chattahoochee River forms part of Alabama's border with Georgia. The Perdido River forms Alabama's eastern border with Florida.

The Gulf Coastal Plain

The Gulf Coastal Plain covers the southern two-thirds of Alabama. The state's lowest point is at sea level along the Gulf of Mexico.

Land in the southeast is called Wiregrass. Tough grasses once grew there. Now, hogs are raised on this land. Peanuts, cotton, and corn grow there.

Swampy land lies in the southwest. Cypress trees and alligators live in the swamps. Oil and natural gas lie under the southwest's land.

Major rivers flow south through the western plain. They include the Tombigbee, Alabama, and Mobile rivers.

Other Gulf Coastal Lands

The Black Belt is part of the Gulf Coastal Plain. It cuts across the middle of the plain. This land has rich, black clay. Cotton fields once covered the land. Now, grasses grow on it. Dairy and beef cattle graze there.

Pine forests grow on the northern plain. The land there has rolling hills.

Swampy land lies in southwestern Alabama.

The Appalachian Highland

Alabama's Appalachian Highland is northeast of the Gulf Coastal Plain. This area is the southernmost part of the Appalachian Mountains.

The state's highest point is in the Appalachian Highland. It is Cheaha Mountain. This mountain rises 2,407 feet (734 meters) above sea level.

The Coosa and Tallapposa are major rivers in the highland. They provide hydroelectric power for nearby cities. Hydroelectric means electricity that is produced by using water.

Two national forests are on the highland. They are Bankhead National Forest and Talladega National Forest.

Coal, iron ore, and limestone lie underground. They provide material for making steel.

The northeastern highland has hog and poultry farms. Cotton, hay, and vegetables grow there.

The Tennessee Valley

The Tennessee Valley covers most of northern Alabama. The Tennessee River twists across the Tennessee Valley land.

Some of Alabama's largest lakes are on the Tennessee River. They include Guntersville, Wheeler, and Wilson. Bass and catfish swim in these lakes.

Alabama Geographical Features

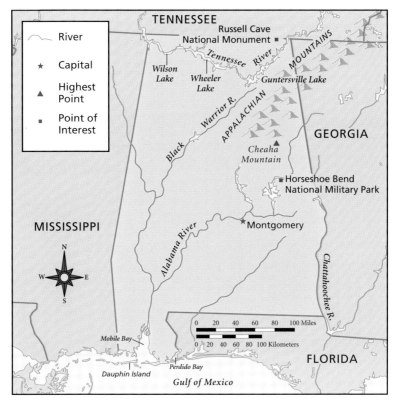

Manufacturing cities grew up along the Tennessee River. The river valley's land is good for farming.

Climate

Alabama's summers are hot and humid. Humid means the air is heavy with moisture. Most winter days are warm. Small amounts of snow may fall in the northern part of the state.

The Gulf Coast receives a lot of rain each year. Hurricanes sometimes hit the coast.

Chapter 3
The People

Alabama is a growing state. Between 1990 and 1994, nearly 180,000 people moved there.

Many of the newcomers were African Americans. Some found jobs in Alabama's cities. Others returned to their hometowns to retire.

Other people have retired in Alabama, too. Most of them are from Mississippi or other southern states. Eastern Mobile Bay is a favorite retirement area.

European Ethnic Groups

Alabama's first European settlers were French. They founded Mobile in 1702. In 1704, Mobile

Alabama grew when many African Americans moved to Birmingham and other cities.

Alabama's settlers built large farms called plantations.

held North America's first Mardi Gras. Mobile still celebrates this French holiday. It takes place eight weeks before Easter.

In the early 1800s, U.S. settlers moved into Alabama. Most of the settlers had English, Scotch-Irish, and German backgrounds. They traveled from Virginia, the Carolinas, Georgia, and Tennessee. They built farms and cotton plantations in Alabama. A plantation is a large farm.

In the late 1800s, European immigrants arrived. German farmers and businesspeople founded Cullman. Italians planted rice and vegetables near

Daphne. Miners came from Scotland and Ireland. They found jobs in coal mines near Birmingham.

Today, about 71 percent of Alabamans have Scotch-Irish, English, or other European backgrounds.

African Americans

About 26 percent of Alabamans are African American. In the past, their families were slaves. Alabama's first African slaves arrived at Mobile Bay in 1721. They worked on rice plantations near Mobile.

By 1860, Alabamans owned 435,080 slaves. The slaves made up 45 percent of Alabama's population. They had hard lives. Many worked on cotton plantations in the Black Belt.

After the Civil War (1861-1865), all the slaves were freed. In the early 1890s, Alabama passed new laws. They limited the rights of African Americans. Thousands moved to northern states.

In the 1960s, Alabama's African Americans worked for civil rights. By the 1980s, Alabama had changed. African Americans started returning to the state. Some have been elected to local government positions.

Native Americans

The Creek, Cherokee, Chickasaw, and Choctaw people once lived in Alabama. They built log homes. The Cherokee used a written language.

In the 1830s, the U.S. government made them leave. Some Creek refused to leave. Today, they are called the Poarch Creek people.

The Poarch Creek Reservation is near Atmore. Tourists visit the reservation's bingo palace. They also attend the Thanksgiving Day powwow.

Today, more than 20,000 Native Americans live in Alabama. The Creek are the largest group. Some Cherokee and Choctaw also live in Alabama.

Other Ethnic Groups

About 75,600 Hispanic Americans live in Alabama. Many of them have Mexican, Puerto Rican, or Cuban backgrounds.

More than 31,000 Asian Americans live in Alabama. Most of them have Chinese, Indian, Korean, or Vietnamese backgrounds.

Many Poarch Creek live on a reservation near Atmore.

Chapter 4

Alabama History

The first people arrived in Alabama about 11,000 years ago. They lived in caves in the northeast.

Other early people built burial mounds in northwestern Alabama. By 1500, the Cherokee, Chickasaw, Choctaw, and Creek lived throughout the state.

Europeans in Alabama

Spanish explorers first sailed into Mobile Bay in 1519. In 1702, two French brothers founded Mobile. This was Alabama's first permanent European town.

In 1763, England gained control of much French land. This included Alabama. England already had 13 colonies along the Atlantic Ocean.

Early people built mounds in northwestern Alabama.

The 22nd State

In 1783, Alabama became part of the United States. This new nation had once been England's 13 colonies.

Settlers started moving into Alabama. In the early 1800s, thousands of settlers poured into Alabama. Many built farms in the east. Others settled in the Black Belt. They started huge cotton plantations.

Little by little, the Native Americans were forced to give up their land. By 1839, only a few remained in Alabama.

In 1819, Alabama became the 22nd state. The capital moved from Huntsville to Cahaba to Tuscaloosa. In 1846, Montgomery became the permanent state capital.

King Cotton

By the 1830s, cotton was Alabama's major crop. Alabama's land and climate were just right for growing cotton. Cotton was so important that people called it King Cotton.

Cotton farmers needed many workers to work in cotton fields. Paid workers would have cost a lot of money. The farmers bought slaves instead. Cotton and slavery were tied together.

The capitol building in Montgomery was built in 1851.

The Civil War and Reconstruction
In the mid 1800s, states' rights and slavery divided the United States. People in the south wanted to increase the power of state governments. They also feared that the U.S. government would outlaw slavery.

Eleven Southern states seceded from the Unites States. In February 1861, Southern leaders met in Montgomery. They formed the Confederate States of America. This led to the Civil War (1861-1865).

In 1864, the Confederates lost the Battle of Mobile Bay. In 1865, they were defeated at Selma and Montgomery. The South surrendered in April 1865. The war ended. All the slaves were freed.

The Southern states had to write new constitutions. They had to give African-American men voting rights. Once they had done that, they could rejoin the Union. Alabama was admitted to the Union again in 1868.

Tenant Farming and New Industries

After the war, Alabama's landowners broke up their plantations. African Americans and poor whites became tenant farmers. A tenant farmer is one who rents land to farm and pays the rent in crops.

In the late 1800s, cities sprung up in northern Alabama. They included Birmingham, Bessemer, and Gadsden. These cities became centers for iron and steel production.

World Wars and Depression

In 1917, the United States entered World War I (1914-1918). Mobile's shipyards built boats for the navy. Alabama's mills made cotton for uniforms.

The entire country suffered during the Great Depression (1929-1939). Prices for crops dropped.

People act out the Battle of Selma which took place in 1865.

Steel mills closed. Many Alabamans lost their jobs. In 1933, the U.S. government started a new program. It was called the Tennessee Valley Authority (TVA). The TVA provided jobs building dams on the Tennessee River.

In 1941, the United States entered World War II (1939-1945). Mobile's shipyards built 196 ships. The Redstone Arsenal company in Huntsville made weapons.

Civil Rights Movement

Since the 1890s, the Southern states had practiced segregation. Segregation kept African Americans and whites apart. They went to separate schools, restaurants, and parks. African Americans had to sit in the back seats of buses. The South also took away African Americans' voting rights.

The civil rights movement started in Alabama in the 1950s. Montgomery's African Americans boycotted city buses after Rosa Parks was arrested. She would not give up her bus seat to a white passenger. Boycott means to refuse to buy or use something as a way of expressing disapproval. African Americans also marched from Selma to Montgomery for their voting

The Civil Rights Memorial honors those who died fighting for equal rights.

rights. In 1954, the Supreme Court ruled that segregation in public schools was against the U.S. Constitution. But segregation did not end for several more years.

More Changes

In 1960, Alabama became an urban state. More people lived in cities than in the country.

By the 1990s, Alabama's cities had attracted high-tech businesses. Many of them made computers. Others did medical research.

Chapter 5

Alabama Business

Manufacturing is Alabama's largest industry. Taken together, however, service industries employ the most people. Farming, mining, and forestry are important, too.

Service Industries

Trade and shipping are major Alabama service industries. Mobile is the state's only port city. It is the nation's 15th busiest port. Ships tie up at its docks. They carry goods from Alabama's factories, farms, and mines.

Millions of tourists visit Alabama each year. They spend more than $3 billion in the state. Restaurants, hotels, and museums receive much of this money.

Tourism is one of Alabama's major industries.

Alabama has thousands of government workers. Many of them teach in Alabama's public schools. Others work at military bases.

Manufacturing

Factories throughout Alabama make paper goods. These are Alabama's leading manufactured products.

Mobile and Decatur make chemicals used in farming. Birmingham produces steel. Computer hardware and software are made in Huntsville.

Alabama's textile mills make yarn, thread, and cloth. Many small towns have clothing factories.

Agriculture

Alabama's leading crop is soybeans. Peanuts and pecans are important crops in southern Alabama. Cotton grows throughout the state. Northern Alabama farmers grow strawberries, peaches, and pears.

Chickens, beef cattle, and hogs are raised in Alabama. Some farmers also raise bees.

Mining, Forestry, and Fishing

Coal and limestone are mined near Birmingham. Oil and natural gas come from wells in

Companies drill for oil in the Gulf of Mexico near Alabama.

southwestern Alabama. The state is also a leading producer of bauxite. Aluminum comes from bauxite.

Large pine forests cover much of Alabama. Yellow pine is used to make paper and lumber.

Alabama fishers catch many shrimp, oysters, and blue crabs. They come from the Gulf of Mexico. Catfish are raised in specially made ponds.

Chapter 6

Seeing the Sights

Alabama's Gulf Coast attracts swimmers to its white sand beaches. Three national forests offer hiking and camping. The state's cities and towns have great museums.

The Gulf Coast

Gulf Shores is on Pleasure Island. It has 32 miles (51 kilometers) of white sand beach. Visitors enjoy swimming and sailing there.

Dauphin Island is west of Gulf Shores. Visitors can fish from an 850-foot-long (259-meter-long) pier. Bayou La Batre is north on the mainland. Many townspeople make their living catching shrimp and oysters there.

Some visitors to Alabama tour the Bellingrath Gardens and Home.

Along Mobile Bay

Bellingrath Gardens and Home is near Theodore. The house has 15 rooms. It stands in the middle of a 65-acre (26-hectare) garden.

Mobile is north of Theodore. Mobile Bay's first fort has been rebuilt. This is Fort Conde. The French built it in 1724. Today, guides at the fort wear French clothing from the 1700s.

The USS *Alabama* Battleship Memorial Park is in Mobile. The *Alabama* served in World War II. Visitors go there to learn about life at sea during wartime.

Point Clear is on the east side of Mobile Bay. Its Grand Hotel was once a Confederate hospital. Now it is a resort. Guests play tennis and golf.

Southeastern Alabama

The Conecuh National Forest is on the Florida border. A 20-mile (32-kilometer) trail winds through the woods. Hikers walk among dogwood, pine, and magnolia trees.

Enterprise is east of the forest. The Boll Weevil Monument stands there. Boll weevils are beetles that destroyed cotton crops in the early

1900s. Since then, southeastern farmers have also grown other crops.

Dothan is farther east. This is southeast Alabama's largest city. Downtown Dothan is very colorful. Murals cover the sides of buildings. These wall paintings show scenes from Alabama's history.

Central Alabama

Montgomery is near the middle of the state. This city has been the state capital since 1846. The Dexter Avenue King Memorial Baptist Church is in Montgomery. Civil rights leader Martin Luther King Jr. was its pastor. From his church, King directed many civil rights protests.

Auburn is northeast of Montgomery. Auburn University is there. This school has produced more astronauts than any other college.

Prattville is northwest of Montgomery. The Buena Vista Mansion stands near town. This is a plantation house. It has a 24-foot (7-meter) circular staircase.

Selma is west of Prattville. In 1965, King led marchers across the Edmund Pettus Bridge. This was a march for African-American voting rights. It ended in Montgomery.

Tuscaloosa is northwest of Selma. It is home to the University of Alabama. The Crimson Tide athletic teams play there.

Tuskegee is east of Montgomery. It is home to Tuskegee University. In 1881, Booker T. Washington founded this college for African Americans. George Washington Carver did experiments there. He made products from peanuts and sweet potatoes.

Horseshoe Bend National Military Park is north of Tuskegee. Andrew Jackson defeated the Creek people there in 1814. Later, he was elected the seventh president of the United States.

Northern Alabama

Talladega is northwest of Horseshoe Bend. The Talladega Superspeedway holds stock car races. Talladega National Forest is east of town.

Birmingham is west of Talladega. This is Alabama's largest city. The Alabama Jazz Hall of Fame is there. The Alabama Sports Hall of Fame is there as well. The city is also home to the Civil Rights Institute. Visitors go there to learn about the nation's civil rights struggle.

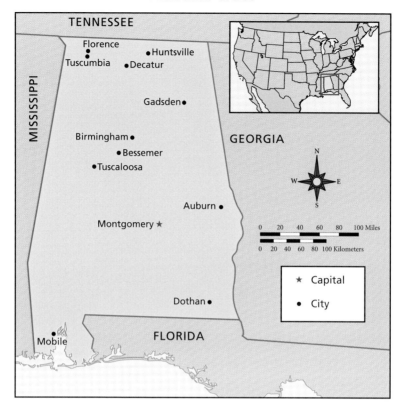

Tuscumbia and Florence are in the northwest corner of the state. In Tuscumbia, visitors can see Helen Keller's home. The W. C. Handy Home is in Florence. Handy was a jazz musician. Visitors to his home can see his handwritten sheet music.

Russell Cave National Monument is in the state's northeast corner. Alabama's first people lived in this cave. Today, visitors can see their tools and weapons.

Alabama Time Line

9000 B.C.—The first people enter Alabama.

A.D. 1500—Creek, Chickasaw, Choctaw, and Cherokee people are living in Alabama.

1519—Spanish explorer Alonso Álvarez de Piee is the first European to enter Mobile Bay.

1540—Hernando de Soto and his forces kill 2,000 Choctaw near Mobile.

1699—Pierre Le Moyne claims the land for France.

1702—Pierre and Jean Baptiste Le Moyne establish Mobile, Alabama's first European town.

1763—England gains Alabama's land from France.

1780—Spain seizes Mobile.

1783—The United States gains Alabama from England.

1813—The U.S. Army captures Mobile from Spain.

1813-1814—The Creek War ends, and the Creek give up most of their Alabama land to the United States.

1819—Alabama becomes the 22nd state.

1830-1836—The Choctaw, Chickasaw, and Cherokee give up their land in Alabama and begin moving to Oklahoma on the Trail of Tears.

1861—Alabama secedes from the Union; the Confederacy's first capital is Montgomery; the Civil War starts.

1865—The Civil War ends; Confederate troops in Mobile and Montgomery surrender.

1868—Alabama rejoins the Union.

1901—A new state constitution takes away voting rights from most African Americans in Alabama.

1933—The Tennessee Valley Authority is formed, bringing electricity and flood control to Alabama.

1955-1956—Montgomery's African Americans boycott city buses after Rosa Parks is arrested for not giving up her seat to a white passenger.

1960—The George C. Marshall Space Flight Center opens in Huntsville.

1964—Governor George Wallace tries to stop African Americans from attending the University of Alabama.

1965—Martin Luther King Jr. leads a march from Selma to Montgomery for voting rights.

1978-1980—The University of Alabama wins the Sugar Bowl three years in a row.

1979—Richard Arrington Jr. becomes Birmingham's first African-American mayor.

1984—Auburn University wins the Sugar Bowl.

1994—Heather Whitestone of Birmingham is crowned Miss America.

1995-1996—Fires destroy several African-American churches in Alabama.

1997—A Mercedes-Benz plant opens in Vance.

Famous Alabamans

Hank Aaron (1934-) Baseball player who holds the record for home runs (775) and for runs batted in (2,297); born in Mobile.

Ralph Abernathy (1926-1990) Baptist minister and civil rights leader who led the Poor People's March to Washington, D.C.; born in Linden.

Nell Carter (1949-) Actress and singer who won a Tony Award for her role in *Ain't Misbehavin'*; born in Birmingham.

Nat King Cole (1919-1965) Singer and songwriter who is known for the song "Unforgettable"; born in Montgomery.

Winston Groom (1943-) Novelist who wrote *Forrest Gump*, which is set in southern Alabama.

W. C. Handy (1873-1958) Composer who is known as the Father of the Blues; born in Florence.

Kate Jackson (1949-) Television actress who starred in "Charlie's Angels" and "Scarecrow and Mrs. King"; born in Birmingham.

Mae Jemison (1956-) First African-American woman in space (1992); born in Decatur.

Helen Keller (1880-1968) Blind and deaf author and lecturer; worked to educate people with disabilities; born in Tuscumbia.

Coretta Scott King (1927-) Civil rights leader and widow of Martin Luther King Jr.; works for the rights of all people; born near Marion.

Harper Lee (1926-) Pulitzer prize-winning author whose book *To Kill a Mockingbird* is set in a small Alabama town; born in Monroeville.

Carl Lewis (1961-) Track and field athlete who won nine gold medals during the Olympic Games in 1984, 1988, 1992, and 1996; born in Birmingham.

Joe Louis (1914-1981) Heavyweight boxing champion (1937-1949); born in Lafayette.

Rosa Parks (1913-) Seamstress who helped start the civil rights movement in 1955; born in Tuskegee.

Julia Tutwiler (1841-1916) Teacher who worked for the right of women to attend the University of Alabama; wrote the words for the state song; born in Tuscaloosa.

George Wallace (1919-) Alabama's governor (1963-1967, 1971-1979, 1983-1987); opposed integration until 1985; born in Clio.

Words to Know

Black Belt—a narrow strip of black clay that runs through central Alabama and Mississippi

boll weevil—a beetle that destroys cotton

boycott—to refuse to buy or use something as a way of expressing disapproval

civil rights—rights that enable all people to take part equally in education, housing, voting, and other public acts

Confederacy—the 11 Southern states that seceded from the Union

hurricane—a strong windstorm that begins over an ocean and causes damage when it hits land

plantation—a large farm

secede—to formally withdraw from a nation or an organization

segregation—a policy of keeping people of different races separate

tenant farmer—a farmer who rents land from a landowner and pays rent in crops

Tennessee Valley Authority (TVA)—a U.S. government agency that was set up to develop the Tennessee River Valley

Wiregrass—land in southeastern Alabama that was once covered by tough grasses; now used for crops

To Learn More

Brown, Dottie. *Alabama*. Hello U.S.A. Minneapolis: Lerner Publications, 1994.

Davis, Lucile. *Alabama*. America the Beautiful. New York: Children's Press, 1999.

Fradin, Dennis B. *Alabama*. From Sea to Shining Sea. Chicago: Children's Press, 1993.

Graves, Kerry A. *The Civil War*. America Goes to War. Mankato, Minn.: Capstone High-Interest Books, 2001.

Shirley, David. *Alabama*. Celebrate the States. New York: Benchmark Books, 2000.

Useful Addresses

Alabama Sports Hall of Fame
2150 Civic Center Boulevard
Birmingham, AL 35203

Bankhead National Forest
P.O. Box 278
Double Springs, AL 35553

Bellingrath Gardens and Home
12401 Bellingrath Gardens Road
Theodore, AL 36582

Civil Rights Memorial
Southern Poverty Law Center
400 Washington Avenue
Montgomery, AL 36101-0548

Horseshoe Bend National Military Park
11288 Horseshoe Bend Road
Daviston, AL 36256

Indian Mound and Museum
1026 South Court Street
Florence, AL 35630

U.S. Space and Rocket Center
One Tranquility Base
Huntsville, AL 35805

Internet Sites

Alabama Department of Archives & History
http://www.archives.state.al.us

Alabama.gov
http://www.alabama.gov

Bellingrath Gardens and Home
http://www.bellingrath.org

Travel.org—Alabama
http://travel.org/alabama.html

Index

African American, 9, 17, 19, 27, 28, 38

Bankhead National Forest, 14
Bellingrath Gardens and Home, 36
Birmingham, 5, 9, 19, 27, 32, 38
Black Belt, 13, 19, 24

Cheaha Mountain, 14
civil rights, 9, 19, 28, 37, 38
Conecuh National Forest, 36
Confederacy, 9, 25, 27
cotton, 13, 14, 18, 19, 24, 27, 32, 36

Dauphin Island, 11, 35

Fort Conde, 36

Gulf of Mexico, 11, 13, 33

Handy, W.C., 39
Horseshoe Bend National Military Park, 38
Huntsville, 5, 7, 24, 28, 32

Keller, Helen, 39
King, Martin Luther Jr, 37

Marshall Space Flight Center, 7

Mobile, 5, 17, 18, 19, 23, 27, 28, 31, 32, 36
Mobile Bay, 11, 17, 19, 23, 27, 36
Montgomery, 4, 5, 9, 24, 25, 27, 28, 37, 38

Native American, 20, 24

Parks, Rosa, 28
Poarch Creek, 20

Russell Cave National Monument, 39

Selma, 9, 27, 28, 37, 38

Talladega National Forest, 14, 38
tenant farmer, 27
Tennessee Valley, 14
Tennessee Valley Authority (TVA), 28
Tuskegee University, 38

University of Alabama, 38
USS *Alabama*, 36